Productivity:

How To Achieve Any Goal In No Time.
Goal Setting Reinvented.
Law of Attraction: Unleash The Secret Power Within and Learn.
How To Manifest More Money, More Love, More Success, More Abundance In No Time.

Ruby Jackson

© 2016

Copyright 2016

by Ruby Jackson- All rights reserved.

This document is geared towards providing exact and reliable information in regards to the topic and issue covered. The publication is sold with the idea that the publisher is not required to render accounting, officially permitted, or otherwise, qualified services. If advice is necessary, legal or professional, a practiced individual in the profession should be ordered.

- From a Declaration of Principles which was accepted and approved equally by a Committee of the American Bar Association and a Committee of Publishers and Associations.

In no way is it legal to reproduce, duplicate, or transmit any part of this document in either electronic means or in printed format. Recording of this publication is strictly prohibited and any storage of this document is not allowed unless with written permission from the publisher. All rights reserved.

The information provided herein is stated to be truthful and consistent, in that any liability, in terms of inattention or otherwise, by any usage or abuse of any policies, processes, or directions contained within is the solitary and utter responsibility of the recipient reader. Under no circumstances will any legal responsibility or blame be held against the publisher for any reparation, damages, or monetary loss due to the information herein, either directly or indirectly.

Respective authors own all copyrights not held by the publisher.

The information herein is offered for informational purposes solely, and is universal as so. The presentation of the information is without contract or any type of guarantee assurance.

The trademarks that are used are without any consent, and the publication of the trademark is without permission or backing by the trademark owner. All trademarks and brands within this book are for clarifying purposes only and are the owned by the owners themselves, not affiliated with this document.

Description

Are you super busy with many tasks to accomplish?

You plan what to do for the day and somehow you fail to remember all the tasks you were to do?

Have you tried putting down on the list those tasks and still you barely make a dent in that list?

Whenever you get down to rest your mind races, reminding you ahead of activities awaiting you to do. Sometimes you even forget to include some tasks on your to-do list. The question is, is your to-do list helpful to you?

Many people are faced with this challenge and often find themselves at crossroads, what to do first with the limited time left. The truth is that most people have a to-do list that does not work them at all.

The research has shown that about 41% of the to-do lists that people prepare often do not get accomplished, let alone the tasks that are not included in the list. Hence, people get overwhelmed and as a result stress chips in.

This book has been written to help you to know how to make an effective to-do list that ensures maximum productivity and to help you evade stress. With a reliable to-do list, you will be able to accomplish more in a day.

This book will help you to avoid the endless cycle of having to postpone your passions, living under stress and even handling emergencies.

Are you ready to change for good? Then grab this copy and start reading…………..

Table of Contents

Description iv

Introduction 1

Chapter 1: How to Determine What You Want 3

Chapter 2: Planning Your Daily Actions 5

Chapter 3: Schedule Your Daily Tasks To Achieve Success 7

Chapter 4: The Power of Your Thoughts 9

Chapter 5: Seven Time Saving Tips 11

Chapter 6: Five Enemies of Productivity 13

Chapter 7: Effectiveness Can Be Learned 17

Chapter 8: Make Your Calendar Your New Best Friend 21

Chapter 9: How Do You Feel? 25

Chapter 10: How to Set Goals 29

Chapter 11: Some Insights About Goals Vs Objectives 37

Chapter 12: 3 Easy Ways to Stick To Your Goals 39

Chapter 13: Keeping Focus On Long-Term Goals And Avoiding Procrastination 41

Chapter 14: To-Do List Power 44

Chapter 15: Positive Attitude Tips - How It Affects Your Success in Life 47

Chapter 16: The Law of Attraction and Making Choices 50

Chapter 17: Habits for Happiness 53

Chapter 18: 5 Ways to Avoid Distractions 56

Chapter 19: Secrets to Get More Done In A Day 58

Chapter 20: Get More Done in Less Time By Batching Your Tasks 61

Chapter 21: Outsourcing -the Right Way to do it 64

Conclusion 68

Introduction

Before you read the actual productivity tips, there is something important worth understanding about personal productivity. And the best way to explain it is by using a metaphor.

Personal productivity is like a building. Now, I'm not an expert on building houses and such but I know this: in order for the building to stand tall and last through various weather conditions, it has to have a solid foundation. Otherwise, the building will collapse.

The foundation has to be solid too, when a person's personal productivity is concerned. If the foundation is missing or one part of it fails, personal productivity becomes just a distant dream.

To have a solid foundation for personal productivity, the following blocks must be in place:

- Proper mindset
- Physical activity
- Optimum nutrition
- Enough sleep

Let's go briefly through each of them, one-by-one.

Proper mindset

Your mind is a very powerful part of you and through your mind, you form your view of the world. Timo Kiander says, 'Your mind also plays a very powerful role in your productivity, since it forms attitudes and these attitudes can eventually turn into action or inaction'.

Thanks for downloading this book. It's my firm belief that it will provide you with all the answers to your questions.

Chapter 1:
How to Determine What You Want

What do you want? When we talk about getting a clear image of what we want, and holding that clear image in our mind, what does that mean?

You might tell me you want a million dollars in the bank or to double your salary. You ought to get a degree or train for a new career. But what is behind that desire?

More often than not the reasons are things like wanting to provide for my family, to buy a new car or get that home you have always wanted. Or maybe it's going on a vacation, taking a month off work or being able to be closer to someone you love.

So what is it that you want? Is a big pile of money the answer? Is money really at the very heart of your desire? More than likely not. You see it as a means to get what you want, the universe sees it as what you are asking for. YOU are making it a two step process when it only needs to be one. Why not spend your time and mental energy asking for the things that you want?

Spend time seeing yourself in that beautiful home, driving that new car, and being with those you love. The way to get those things will open up for you, and it will probably be in ways you never thought of. This way you go directly to the source, asking for and getting, what you want.

You may still end up with a big pile of money. But the problem with focusing on the money is that we often spend too much time trying to figure out how we will get what we desire. When we try to figure it out for ourselves, we limit the many ways that the Universe can bring it to us, and you slow down the whole process.

People often say they want money as a means of security. But what greater security could there be than being able to manifest what you need whenever you need it. This could be money, but it does not have to be. Be open to getting your answers in new ways.

Wallace Wattles writes in The Science of Getting Rich that **'It is not your part to guide or supervise the creative process. All you have to do with that is to retain your vision, stick to your purpose, and maintain your faith and gratitude.'**

All the pieces of the picture will fall together as they are needed. Bypass the thinking that you need a certain amount of money to have what you want and go directly to the having what you want, not limiting the ways it could come to you.

Chapter 2: Planning Your Daily Actions

The business environment is rapidly changing, offering new and unique challenges that we must adapt to flourish. Advances in technology have provided us with greater efficiency eliminating many of the positions that employees had previously held. This has resulted in an ever-growing task list and a schedule that gets busier by the day; thus necessitating the clear identification of your responsibilities and tasks to simplify your life.

Review your Job Description

It is important to review and update your job description to reflect the changes in the tasks and responsibilities that have occurred. When you define the expectations that you have for yourself, you can take the next step towards properly managing your time. Likewise, having a defined job description in place for your staff makes both your job and their job more effective.

Create a Task Action List

Create a checklist that outlines all of the tasks that you are responsible for. Begin with your job description and list of the corresponding tasks based on required frequency. Next, over a time span of four weeks, track the tasks that you are responsible for completing and add them to the action list.

Accomplishing Your Tasks

Organize your tasks into a document that can easily be followed. We recommend dividing your task list into daily, weekly, monthly, quarterly and yearly lists. These checklists can then be printed out once a month and followed to assist you in completing your tasks. There are many benefits to having this document in place, such as the ability of others to easily step into your position during vacations or when you move to a different position. This document can be adjusted to reflect your individual style and easily translates to other tracking programs such as Outlook.

Chapter 3:
Schedule Your Daily Tasks To Achieve Success

There is a vast difference between scheduling and simple list making. While it is a good thing to have lists because they help to outline the things that need to be done as opposed to the things that do not. On the other hand, a list can be an exasperating reminder of all the work left do accomplish that is still waiting.

Scheduling the task list provides the task a schedule to be performed. Doing this simple action causes thought as to what task will be done and at what time. This might cause the list to change. For example, when using a schedule for the list, tasks that might have been first on the list might be moved down because they take longer. If there is no accounting for time to accomplish the task, there is no idea of a more efficient time of day to get that particular task finished.

If a daily task list has 24 items on it and it takes an hour to perform each task, to achieve a successful completion of that list will leave little time for sleeping, eating, etc. Of course, it's not possible. However, this is how many people make and view their daily task list. These results in frustration at not accomplishing perhaps even part of the list.

Scheduling brings time availability to light and forces the list to change. One of the main reasons people have success and happy, healthy, and can accomplish wonderful things for themselves is that they use our natural ability to think, reason, and plan ahead. This is the key separation between humans and animals. An animal is not created with the ability to reason. The intelligence they have in abundance, but they lack reason.

When considering a daily task list, try instead to schedule each task at a time for a time. Providing enough time to adequately perform the task with room for a little variation. In this manner, the daily tasks are presented against real-time because you have had to consider and reason out each task and how long it will take.

By doing this, you can avoid the stress and frustration of not completing your list or the feelings of being out of control. It also will help to categorize each task. In other words, if there is more time another day, and it can wait, it can be pushed a little further out and something more immediately needful put in its place.

Scheduling your daily tasks might seem to be counterintuitive in that in and of itself it is another task to add. Indeed, if scheduling is new to you, it will be something to become used to doing. Despite that little hurdle, once you develop the good habit of scheduling it will become something that is second nature and an essential tool for your continued success.

Chapter 4: The Power of Your Thoughts

Whatever you think about, dream about, complain about or have any emotion about, you bring more of the same into your life. So the work you need to do is not to monitor every thought that runs through your head, but to direct your thinking in the way you want it to go. To deliberately think about what you want and how you want things to be, and not think about an outcome you do not want. You have to become a deliberate thinker.

Thoughts and emotions are kinds of like a tuning fork. When a tuning fork vibrates at a particular pitch anything around on the same tone or frequency will vibrate. Law of Attraction is activated by the "tune" of your thoughts and emotions and brings to you whatever "frequency" you are sending out.

We are, for the most part, attracted to the people we are vibrating with. People tend to have similar values, ideas, and even economic levels. So one trick to changing your vibration to a higher level is to spend time with people who have what you have or live like you live, even if you do not have it yet. This raises your vibration to that level.

It's not all about having the most stuff or the highest status. It is about bringing yourself up to a level of appreciation to attract more of what you want. No matter what your situation is now, you can change it. You have a life of unlimited possibilities before you.

Our thoughts are the most powerful thing we have. What we think today shapes our future. You have the choice to think a different way, imagine it differently, talk about it differently. One choice can turn your life around.

If you take Law of Attraction seriously, you have to take responsibility for what you say, think and do. You have to give up blaming and complaining and instead take time each day to focus on what you truly want. You can block the flow of what you want by being negative or doubting.

There is a tremendous amount of power in thought. To live the Law of Attraction and make it work for you; you must be intentional about what you are thinking. Don't let yourself dwell on the negative, instead, seek out a solution and focus the things that are good and positive.

Chapter 5: Seven Time Saving Tips

Our time is valuable. It is important to be efficient when working through the recurring tasks that need to be completed each day. By implementing these simple seven-time-saving tips, you can save yourself precious minutes and create a more productive life.

1. Phone Calls

Schedule one or two-time frames each day to return phone calls. Group all of the phone calls that you need to return together and work through them during your scheduled time frame.

Set phone hours. Let people know you are available to answer the phone at a certain time each day. If a client calls outside of this time, allow them to leave a message. This will allow you to concentrate on your work without being interrupted.

2. Emails

To reduce the number of emails going back and forth, be specific and clear. Use bullet points to ensure that the recipient clearly identifies each question or topic.

When scheduling meetings via email, offer three specific meeting times for your recipients to choose from.

3. Mail

Schedule a time on your calendar each day to collect, open, and file your mail. Do not allow your mail to collect on your desk unopened. This will help reduce desk clutter and ensure that you will not miss an opportunity.

4. Filing

Schedule a time at the end of every day to clear your desk and file any papers that you have received. This will allow you to start each morning with a clear desk and help eliminate the pesky problem of stacks of paper.

5. Delegate

Surround yourself with people that you trust. Your staff and associates are there to help you. People are often flattered when they are asked to pitch in and help.

6. Meetings

Create a meeting agenda for every meeting that you schedule. Assign a point person to ensure that the meeting stays on task.

7. Meet by Phone

Do not meet in person unless it is essential. This will enable you to cut down on your travel time and free up your schedule to accomplish more in a day. Instead, schedule a time to "meet" by phone with three-way calling, available through most phone companies, or conference calling. Another way to meet virtually is with Skype, either with a webcam so you can see each other, or without.

Chapter 6: Five Enemies of Productivity

We all want to be successful and make a greater contribution to the world we live and work in. The problem? Life gets in the way. It's the things we do - or don't do - that rob us of the joy of accomplishment and contribution.

You know me and my position on life in general: Live intentionally! Life is way too short to live any other way. One of my favorite quotes is from Peter Drucker: "The only way to get the future you want is to create it." While it's true we're not omnipotent; we do have the ability to think, reason and make good decisions.

One of the ways we can do a better job of living intentionally is to know who our enemies are. Yes, I said enemies. There's more than one and, in most cases, our number one enemy is ourselves.

Here's a short list that, when identified and confronted, can make your life a whole lot more productive.

Un-clarity

I know, it's not a word, but un-clarity means you don't have a clear vision for what you want to accomplish in either the long or short term. You're just waking up each day and taking what life throws your way. I have two words for you: Stop it!

An unfocused mind is a confused mind. Focus! Get clear on what you want to accomplish and why. To make that happen, use my S.M.A.R.T. methodology for drafting a specific vision. How much? By when? These are two good questions to start the process of clarifying what you want to achieve.

Failure to Control Your Calendar

If you don't control your calendar - someone else will. We all have time to give to others, the time we have to spend on someone else's agenda or project, but we can also make time to focus on those few things that matter, personally or professionally - to us. And here's the good news: you only need about 90 minutes a day to make a huge, positive impact on your world and your agenda.

Start with the time you have available on your calendar. Schedule two 45-minute blocks or three 30-minute blocks to work on MIAs (most important activities). Treat those times as though they were a meeting with your boss or most important client. MIA time is a sacred time when it comes to your performance and productivity.

The Myth of Multitasking

I've written about this before. Nothing good happens when you try and do several things at once. The secret to being effective is a concentration of effort. This applies in particular when you need to bear down and focus on details or important data. You'll get more accomplished - in a shorter period - by eliminating distractions and concentrating on one activity or task at a time.

Low Energy Levels

To increase your effectiveness, you'll need to maintain a high degree of energy. Whether your energy is down because of lack of sleep, hunger, or because you're simply out of shape, you need to consider ways to keep your batteries charged. Plan for the amount of sleep you need each night to awaken refreshed and ready to take on the day. There's a variety of energy foods out there that are inexpensive and easy to get your hands on.

Interruptions

After working from home for some years, I'm amazed at how anyone gets anything done in the typical office or workplace. Visiting client sites, I'm struck by how many interruptions most people have to deal with in a given day.

Now, to be fair, many are self-inflicted. More often than not we allow others to drop in and disrupt. Whether it's because we want to be friendly, or a team player, or help others just get away and clear their heads, we'll shoot ourselves in the foot by tolerating interruptions - especially when we're in our MIA time block.

Control the controllable. More often than not, that means taking charge of our day and the events of the day. It means being intentional in the way we deal with our MIAs. Be clear on your real priorities: control the calendar, stop multi-tasking, keep your energy levels high and avoid interruptions.

Chapter 7: Effectiveness Can Be Learned

Effectiveness: the degree to which something is successful in producing the desired result.

Do you want to be successful? If you do, then you're going to have to learn to be effective. And the good news is, effectiveness can be learned.

I've given you the dictionary definition of effectiveness, but now let me give you the bottom line definition: effectiveness is getting the right things done.

Doing a lot of different things at once just means you can multi-task but, in this day and age - who can't? Thanks to incredible technology and attention span no longer than a nano-second, it's relatively easy to do a bunch of stuff all at the same time. Here's the problem, though; multi-tasking and being effective are often mutually exclusive.

If you're interested in learning to be effective instead of being efficient, here are four key skills you'll want to develop:

Time Mastery

You notice I didn't say time management. Time mastery is quite different. Because time is your most limiting and non-renewable resource, mastering the seconds, minutes and hours in your day will be critical for you and your success.

Mastery is about owning your time. It's about realizing you have much more control over your time than you may be giving yourself credit for. It's also about realizing that eighty percent of your productivity will come from twenty percent of your activity. To be effective, you'll need to identify those tasks that will lead to getting the most important things done, personally and professionally. You'll need to learn to make the most of that precious resource - time.

Question: Do you currently behave as though you realize time is the most limiting factor in your life?

Making Your Strengths Productive

You simply cannot afford to take the time to try and improve your weaknesses. Instead, identify your strengths, strengthen them and make them productive. And, figure out a way to work around your weaknesses.

The most effective way to multiply your performance capacity is by making your (unique) strengths productive. No one else has your strengths. Leverage them to give you a performance advantage in the workplace.

Focus on Contribution

The primary role of every employee - in any organization - is to contribute to the success of the enterprise. Mastering your time and playing to your strengths are certainly ways to contribute. I'm sure you can think of other ways as well. Focusing on contribution, instead of just showing up and going through the motions, will put you in the top ten percent of all the employees in your organization - and in the country.

Here's a key question: "What kind of unique contributions can I make that will help make my company a success in this industry?"

Practice Abandonment

The secret of effectiveness lies in the concentration of effort. There is always more to do than time available. Your task is to identify those things that simply do not contribute to the success of the enterprise and abandon them. Yes, give them up. Remember, only twenty percent of what you do contributes to your success. Everything isn't an "A" priority, so figure out what the "As" are and get rid of the rest. Delegate if you can but if you can't, just stop doing them - and see if anyone notices.

Question: Have I taken a hard look at abandoning those things I simply don't have to do? Shouldn't I have an abandonment discussion with my boss?

Effectiveness involves figuring out how to produce the desired result. Whether it's your results or the results your company expects, being effective means achieving them by getting the right things done - personally and professionally.

Chapter 8: Make Your Calendar Your New Best Friend

If you want to increase your performance and productivity, you'll have to learn to use your calendar as a time management tool. You have more control over your time than you give yourself credit for. One of the easiest ways to control your time is by controlling your calendar.

We're all given the same measure of time each day. You have twenty-four hours - which translates to 1,440 minutes - to work with each day. You have the same amount of time as did Michelangelo, Mother Teresa, and Einstein. You have the same number of hours and minutes each day as does Bill Gates or the President of the United States. Your productivity won't be predicated on how much time you have, but rather on how you use that time to complete your most important tasks.

Here's how you can leverage your productivity by leveraging the use of your daily calendar.

Plan Your Work

You start to control your time by planning your day. Take 10-15 minutes every morning to plan your work. Each day is unique. Schedules change, and so do our priorities. Taking time every morning to review your schedule - and schedule priorities - is how you'll start to control your calendar.

Create a Master List - Then Prioritize

We all have important tasks or projects to complete, but not every task or project carries the same priority. Create a "master list" of all of your important tasks and projects. Once the master list is created, prioritize it. By the way, create your master list in pencil. Why? Because things change - including priorities. You'll need to adjust your list and your calendar regularly to address those priority changes.

Use Most Productive Hours - For Your Most Important Tasks

Not only is each day unique but each of us is a unique individual. We're cyclical creatures. Our energy levels peak and wane at different times. Psychologists refer to these emotional peaks and valleys regarding biorhythms. Increasing your performance and productivity means knowing how to use your biorhythms to your advantage. If you're a "morning person," you'll want to schedule important tasks when your energy and attention span is highest. If your energy levels are higher in the afternoon or evening, schedule accordingly.

Incorporate 80/20 Into Your Daily Plan

Using the 80/20 rule makes a lot of sense when it comes to time management. Studies show that 80 percent of your productivity will come from 20 percent of your activity. Twenty percent of an eight-hour day is 96 minutes. Look at your calendar and see if you can calendar 90 minutes to work on your most important project. It doesn't have to be 90 continuous minutes. Schedule three 30-minute segments or two 45-minute blocks of time to deal with your priority project (s).

Just Say "No."

As you plan your day and work your plan, you'll immediately face challenges. The greatest challenge you'll likely face is your coworkers, and perhaps your boss, wanting to make their priorities your priorities. Don't let that happen. With coworkers, it's a little easier to say simply, "I'm sorry, but I don't have time to handle that in the way it deserves. But thanks for thinking of me." If it's your boss, just mention that important project he/she wanted to be completed and asked if this new one has priority.

Start Now!

Hesitancy, fear, and self-doubt all fade with action. Once you have your priority list in order, commit to taking action on the top three. You'll validate that commitment by scheduling time on your calendar to start working on one of your most pressing tasks. Break the task or project into small actions and take those actions at the appropriate time.

Chapter 9: How Do You Feel?

"What we are today comes from our thoughts of yesterday, and our present thoughts build our life of tomorrow: Our life is the creation of our mind."

-Buddha

According to Merriam-Webster, it is a force that brings good fortune or adversity. To me, bad luck is an oxymoron but regardless, being that I'm a bit Irish and with St. Patrick's Day upon us I thought it a good topic to talk about.

As a side note, did you know that the "Luck of the Irish" can be interpreted either way? Some say they were lucky, and some say they were unlucky. But as always it's all about how you interpret anything that makes the difference in how you will experience it. It's the glass half full or half empty kind of thing.

So, let me ask you again: How do you feel? Many times I feel so lucky for so many reasons but believe me when I tell you there are times that I forget how truly lucky I am. I can moan and complain and whine about stuff but it's typically short lived once I come back to my senses.

This should be an excerpt from Confessions of a Positive Person! Positive people aren't supposed to feel anything but upbeat, happy, hopeful and positive, right? Well yes, you would think so but that isn't always the case, even for us proclaimed positive types.

We all have our share of frustrations, heartache, disappointments and adversities too. There are days that you wish you could do over, days you wish you could entirely forget about, and there are days you wish would never end. Sadly, most people don't experience the latter often enough.

But, it is when these negative feelings that haunt each and every one of our lives come knocking at your front door that you have to decide whether you are going to invite them in for a very short visit or have them check in for an extended stay. Some people allow these unwanted feelings stay so long they don't know how to get them to leave.

The difference between positive and negative people is mainly one thing. It is what they think. And as you all know by now we choose what we think. And what we think about we bring about! Sure, you can get cranky, irritated and teed off, who doesn't? But what makes the biggest difference is how long you allow those kinds of feelings and emotions to hang out with you. And again...therein lies the difference.

So when I ask you how you feel, remember you choose how you are going to feel by what you choose to think about. Let me break it down in its most simplistic form.

Your beliefs about something create your thoughts about it. Your thoughts about it create how you are going to feel about it. How you feel will be how you experience it. Beliefs → Thoughts → Feelings → Experience. So if you're feeling lucky, happy, grateful or whatever it's all about what thoughts you choose to interpret whatever is going on in your life.

The last numerous months my mom has been very sick, and I can't imagine losing her, but I know that someday it is inevitable. It is something I try to avoid thinking about but the other night I got on a crying jag about it because the thought of loss was so overwhelming. I realized that this pain is just a glimpse of what I will experience when that day comes.

But I also realized that it is a part of the process called grief. And as afraid as I am about going through it I also know that I will move through it. So, no matter what's happening in your life choose how you view it. Don't be so mad about stuff you have no control over and do something about what you can control. Stop living with regrets and start to focus on your blessings. Quit living in the past and wishing things were different begin to live for today and wish for the best instead.

How you feel right this very second is all about what you are thinking. I feel lucky! I feel so fortunate that I still have some time with my mom, that I can touch people's lives with my work and that I live with more of a positive outlook than a negative one. And do you want to know why I do, because that is what I choose!

Chapter 10: How to Set Goals

Your individual goals should be properly termed objectives. Objectives should be aligned with your manager's, your department's, your office, and your Company. Alignment ensures all effort is going toward the result of achieving the goal. This will support the mission and make the vision a reality. It all flows in the same direction together. Anyone that has ever rolled their eyes at this process, or performance management overall, does not understand that it is the root of your Company's and your personal success.

The effective objective setting means that each employee has measurable individual objectives that are focused on helping the Company's overall goals. Each employee should have a clear understanding of his or her performance accountabilities. All employees should have a clear understanding of how performance against these objectives will be evaluated and rewarded.

Setting Objectives: Planning & Measuring Results

Your objectives should reflect how you could drive goals, profitability, and related business results about your role within your Company. They should be measurable so that you and your manager can gauge your accomplishments. Always use this rule of thumb: select two or three objectives in each of these critical business areas.

Create an action plan for each objective. Next, are the steps to accomplish each objective. The acronym SMART (you've seen it a million times!) is not a cliché. It's truly an effective way of building objectives that support the organization and help you stay on track. For each objective and step of the action plan follow these SMART guidelines:

Objectives
Action Plan Steps

Specific:

Is the objective completely understood between you and your manager?

Example: Decrease or remove potential customers' resistance to buying our product, leading to a 20 percent increase in sales closed within in six months or less.

Map out specific activities that need to be completed.; these are tactical:

* Advertise in 10 magazines per month.
* Distribute product samples to 20 clients weekly.
* Offer free online seminars to potential clients; one per month.

Measurable:

How will you know when it's been achieved? Will you be able to measure the degree to which it's been achieved?

Example: Increase product market share by 13% by the end of 2010.

Put measures around each tactic that will help achieve the overall objective.

* Distribute free samples or discount coupons at high school football games.
* Sponsor an event attended by teens by the end of the quarter.

Ambitious:

Is this objective a stretch? Is it too little? Too much?

Example: Realize an expense cost savings of 25% by year-end.

Objectives that stretch outside of our comfort zone are what take us to the next level. If last year's cost savings was 25% - can you stretch it to 30%? The timeframe in which you can reach the stretch goal? Be realistic, but push yourself.

Relevant:

Is the objective aligned with the objectives of my manager/department/company?

Example: Become the employer of choice in an appropriate industry by returning correspondence with all applicants within 48 hours.

The objective has to be in alignment with each of the other levels of objectives to be relevant. Remember that each person's success is a success for the Company.

- Build a tracking database by October 31;
- Start tracking all applicants by November 15;
- Create and distribute an automated email for applicants by November 30.

Timely:

By when must I achieve the objective?

Each tactic in the action plan should have a time around it as highlighted in orange above.

Measuring Success: Measuring the effectiveness of objectives is not always an easy task. To simplify it, ask yourself this question - is the measurement for the objective crystal clear to you and your manager? A great measure of success is both concise and memorable, integrating the sales, revenue, and production goals you are striving to achieve.

Most importantly, your measure of success needs. Typically, measures fall into the following categories:

Activity Based

- Meet with ten clients per month.
- Attend CE classes
- Perform all duties as directed

Cost Based

- Cut expenses by $100K
- Increase revenue by $50K per quarter
- Reduce paper waste by $5K

Percent Based

- Decrease defects by 10%
- Increase customer satisfaction by 3%
- Grow profit on my business by 5%

Number Based

- Increase new clients by 15 per quarter
- Get at least 1 employee into the management training program

Other Measures

- Time saved
- Productivity increased
- Customer Feedback

Activity based measurements are not effective when they are the only measures of objective success. An employee could be engaged in all the wrong activity and not getting the desired result. I've seen many employees at all levels of an organization measure activity and not anything else because they don't know how to create effective objectives. There are three components to completing your part of the individual objectives & action plan:

Learn

- Company Goals
- Strategic Initiatives
- Department Goals
- Manager Objectives
- Review your company's PM process and the forms associated with it

Plan

- Read this guide thoroughly
- Schedule a meeting with your manager to discuss, refine and agree on your objectives
- Meet with your HR Manager to help you understand the process

Act

- Complete your company created objective forms
- Send your draft to your manager so he can review it before your meeting
- Prepare your action plan for the meeting
- Ask for resources to help you achieve your objectives

Learn, Plan, Act.

Learn. After gathering your Company's mission and vision statements, it's time to review and understand the department's goals as well as your manager's objectives. Regardless of whether your manager has given you their objectives or not, it is strongly recommended you complete your own with the information you have. Collect all the forms that apply to your Company's performance management process; these forms could include a balanced scorecard, self-appraisal, formal year-end appraisal, definition of rates, and development planning.

Plan. Starting by reading this guide will help you have a deeper understanding of what performance management is all about and how your Company measures up. Knowledge is power and the more information you have, the more confidence you will gain which will help you manage your career path. Now is the time to ask your manager for a copy of her objectives so that you can draft your own based on theirs.

Schedule an objective-setting meeting with your manager (for at least one hour) to discuss, refine, and agree to your objectives.

Act. Complete a draft of your objective form (we will cover how to write effective objectives in the next section.) Send your draft objectives and action plan (which we will also cover in the next section) to your manager so she can review it before your meeting. Identify what support you'll need from your manager and other team members to achieve the objectives you've prepared. What resources will you need? What feedback will you want? Prepare this for your meeting with your manager and present a business case for getting the resources you need, especially if the resources are outside the norm (i.e. training, seminars, travel - anything that will cost money.) Meet with your manager to get agreement on your objectives and an action plan. Lastly, submit your completed form to 1) your manager, and 2) to Human Resources to be placed in your personnel file.

Important Note: This is a working document that should frequently be reviewed for updates and changes. One common misconception about objectives is that once they're written for the year they are set in stone. Nothing could be farther from the truth. Keep the document where you can see it, read it and edit it as you need to. This will keep you motivated to complete your objectives.

Chapter 11: Some Insights About Goals Vs Objectives

Goals vs. objectives? Some people get confused with these two. Some thought of these as words with the same meaning. Both words are pertaining to achieving something or being able to reach an aspiration. Well, in every plan, there must be a goal. And in every goal, there must be objectives. Goals and objectives must work hand in hand. Your actions must be directly towards the goal, and those actions must get your objectives done.

The goal in particular has a broader scope. The efforts that you have to exert to achieve it might be unmeasurable. It also differs in objective when it comes to its time frame. Goals are mostly achieved after a long process. It comes with a long-term planning as well. Goals can also be defined as a general intention of a certain individual, group, organization, institution, or company. There may be a lot of efforts and a lot of change of plans that might happen as you go about achieving a goal. Some unexpected events might also affect the time frame of your goal, and as has been said, goals might be unmeasurable.

On the other hand, objectives are more specific. You can easily pin point the things that you can do to achieve a target. Objectives are easy to measure and their time frame is short. If you analyze, goals vs. objectives, you will realize that objectives are part of the things that you will do to achieve a goal. Objectives are things which are set to achieve in a shorter period.

Goals vs. objectives, these two are different from each other, but they have the same purpose, and it is achieving something. Achieving a certain thing for an individual or an organization. And again, they must work hand in hand for a certain individual or organization to reach the peak of success. They are not hard to achieve as long as you will stick to your plan and if you will keep your eyes to what you want to achieve. Your direction must always be on the way where you can have the success. If you switch plans, you have to make sure that your objectives and goals can still be realized.

With the question goals vs. objectives, your objectives must support your goals. When you can finish an objective, that means that you are one step ahead of achieving your goal. And you have to keep going on accomplishing each task to finish each objective. The process has to keep going and in no time, you'll just realize that you are getting close to your desired goal. Goals vs. objectives should not be a blur to you. If you can distinguish these two and can execute plans, you'll reach your target. And who knows it might be in a shorter period. With all the questions about goals vs. objectives, they still boil down to one thing, and that is achieving the peak of success.

Chapter 12: 3 Easy Ways to Stick To Your Goals

Stick To Your Goals - Make them a priority

Of course, this is a lot easier if your goals are in line with your values.

If you want to lose weight, stop thinking of losing. That's tip 1. We don't like to lose; we like to win or achieve something. Gain new clothes, shoot for a better dress size or aim for more activity. Make it a positive goal, not a losing goal.

Tip 2: Why do you want this goal? If you don't know why, or it's not a reason that resonates with you, you won't achieve your goals. That's why most goals fail, even if you use the SMART system. Or, you feel sleazy gaining the goal because you had to violate some part of your values to get it. Make sure your goals are in line with your values.

Tip 3: Get accountability. Sometimes, all you need is a partner to keep you in line. Sometimes, you need someone bigger. That's why I help people lose weight so successfully: I keep people accountable for what they eat. They need to justify why they ate certain foods and come up with better solutions.

Goals are great. We all need to have them. But, we can't sacrifice our values just to get our goals.

Sticking to your goals starts way before you set your goals.

Do you set SMART goals? Well, you just may set yourself up for failure. SMART goals focus on the results, not you, not your values, not your family. They only want you to succeed.

Now, if succeeding is all that matters, set SMART goals. But for most of us, we want to have our goals fit into our lives, be at peace with the process and enjoy the results.

Set value based goals. When you choose value-based goals, you align your system of values with your goal. Every choice you make on the way to achieving your goal is balanced against the values you hold dear.

For example, I value being on time. For that, I will make the choice of doing a task, such as an exercise, before leaving for an appointment or skipping it. If I have time, I exercise, if not, I reschedule. My value dictates my end results and my choices.

Look back at your goals. Do they align with your values? If not, review your goals, make them positive, value-based, and personal to you, your family and your life.

Chapter 13: Keeping Focus On Long-Term Goals And Avoiding Procrastination

Many individuals fail to accomplish their long-term goals mainly because their interest simply wanes in the long run. Their focus shifts and their enthusiasm fades away as other more urgent issues come along the way. Long-term goals seem to become either less important or unrealistic as time goes by. In most cases, the principal culprit for the fading impetus is usually procrastination.

Avoid distractions

Procrastination results to the piling up of tasks, making it highly stressful and overwhelming to accomplish goals. Case in point is a real estate agent who might procrastinate in making follow ups of prospective clients. The required monthly or quarterly sales quota may not be met as a result of the procrastination.

Meeting quarterly sales quotas, saving fixed amount of money per month, submitting research papers on time and losing weight are some examples of short-term goals that lead to accomplishing long-term goals. Financial stability, earning a college degree and life-long health are the corresponding long-term goals. The short-term goals or objectives serve as the baby steps in ultimately accomplishing the more difficult long-term goals.

Individuals will be unable to focus on lifetime goals if they cannot resist the urge to procrastinate. Distractions are everywhere and sometimes are very appealing. For instance, a student reviewing for an important exam may be distracted to go on a date or party all night. Peer pressure, pleasurable prospects, laziness, and stress are some of the most common sources of distractions.

Anticipate obstacles

Any worthwhile goal will always need effort and investment of resources. Worthwhile long-term goals are particularly difficult to accomplish because there are many factors to consider. Obstacles will be present along the way. Although not all obstacles or contingencies can be clearly anticipated, it is very crucial to anticipate challenges that may appear.

Anticipating obstacles will allow room for better preparation and adjustments. One cannot easily be caught off-guard or overwhelmed by problems if there are contingency plans in place. For example, a fruit stand owner must anticipate the price fluctuations and seasonal or climate-related changes that may affect the supply of fruits.

Visualize success

Sustaining motivation and keeping the focus on the long-term goals may seem daunting without the prospect of success. Visualizing success is crucial in sustaining the drive. People who are not very confident that they will succeed are less likely to accomplish their dreams.

Visualizing success will allow individuals to be highly specific about their goals. It will help them gain confidence and insights on what steps to take. It is about formulating a directed action plan that is centered on the goals.

Chapter 14: To-Do List Power

Many people are now turning to their To-Do list to enable them get more done than usual. Many people tend to have a long To-Do list that rolls over day after another without getting the things listed done. There is a solid reason for this.

The reason this happens is you don't consciously know what's underneath the items on your list. The list is coming led with actions, good ideas, and projects. Some of which you should be doing because it's your job or role and some of which you should not be doing at all. The challenge is you may not be conscious of what the sub-actions are that need to be done to check off a particular item. The not knowing causes the anxiety and procrastination. People will do just about anything to avoid uncertainty.

The fix is to get the items on the right list. I'll share with you four key lists you may want to consider creating to enable you to stay focused and work from just your one To-Do list and thereby get more accomplished.

The only thing that should be on your To-Do list are single action items you know you can do. Keep in mind you can't do a project, although you can do actions that lead to the completion of a project. Consider having a To-Do list that contains only true action items. Consider another separate list titled: Projects.

Pull out your current list. You know, the one that has been rolling over and over. Next to each of the items that are single action items, write an 'A' for action. Next to the items that take more than one action or step to complete, write a 'P' for a project. Keep the 'A' items on your To-Do list and transfer the 'P' items to the newly created Projects list. Then, for each item on the Project list, think through and identify what actions are needed to complete each project. Post those actions items to your To-Do list. This will obviously increase your To-Do list. It may seem like more work. Stick with me here.

Keep in mind; time exists, so you don't have to do everything all at once. This process will greatly reduce any overwhelm you may have been experiencing.

To get your power back create two more lists. One titled: Another Good Idea and another one called: Not To-Do. Now comb through your first two lists - Actions and Projects. Pull from each of those lists the items that seemed like a good idea at the time you entered them but may not be moving the genius meter anymore. Move those over to the Another Good Idealist. You can always go back to your AGI list and pull items back onto the To-Do list when and if appropriate.

Hopefully, as you transfer items onto the AGI, your To-Do list is reducing in volume. To continue bringing your To-Do list down to a manageable inventory of items, identify those actions that really won't make a difference in supporting your goals if they don't get done. Park those items on the Not To-Do list. Notice the tasks and activities that suck your time throughout your days and write those down on your NTD list too.

To take back your power and start getting more done, make it habit of taking the time to recalibrate your new lists weekly. Update your To-Do list daily. Each evening as you end your day identify the 3-6 items from your To-Do list that must get done the next day. Imagine having completed them successfully. The following day stays focused on getting them done. As you have those great ideas of new things to do park them on the AGI list and when their time is right to move them to your Project or To-Do list. Check yourself periodically during the day to make sure you have not drifted into doing anything on your NTD list.

Give this process a couple of weeks and notice how much more you get done and how much more in control you feel. Make it up, make it fun & make it happen!

Chapter 15: Positive Attitude Tips - How It Affects Your Success in Life

If you are someone who is struggling to stay positive and get positive results in all areas of your life. Then read this chapter on positive attitude tips. It has helped many people make a positive difference in their life, and it can help you have better results in your life.

Learning to Keep a positive attitude is one of the 9 key success habits that successful people use to have success in reaching their goals and dreams.

Nine key habits play a major part in the outcome of everything that you do. Your attitude is one of the most important habits you need to be practicing. It truly has a big impact on how you perceive life and the results that you get in life. Because if you have a bad attitude most of the time, then you already have one strike against you when trying to accomplish something. When you have a poor attitude you cannot see the purpose of what you are doing and to make matters worse you do not even care.

When you a bad attitude you have to overcome all the negativity every time you do something. That takes a lot of energy, and it will drain the life right out of you.

It also takes more time to do something when you have a poor attitude versus when you have a positive attitude. Also, people, in general, do not want to be around others when they have a bad attitude. They try their best to avoid being around negative people at all cost. This whole scenario is so counterproductive and depressing, and it ends up hurting your life.

When you have a positive attitude, you look forward to life and everything you do. That is why having a positive attitude is essential to your happiness and success.

The important thing that you need to know and realize is that your attitude is all controlled by you. It is a choice whether you have a good or bad attitude.

1. You can start by making it a habit to be aware of how you are thinking and feeling throughout the day. It is best to start doing this as soon as you get up in the morning and continue monitoring your attitude throughout the day.

2. Once you realize that you have a poor attitude, start to change it consciously to one that is a good attitude.

Here are a few things I suggest you can try to help do change your attitude. You can try reading a book or watching a movie on something positive or funny. You can call or hang out with a family member or friend who is upbeat. You can spend time with your pet or take a walk.

3 Stay away from people you know who usually have a bad attitude. Because they will only have a bad effect on you.

When I started learning and applying success habits in my everyday life. It forever changed all areas of my life for the better.

Remember that your attitude is a choice and only you can determine whether it is positive or negative.

It is important to keep your attitude positive to help you get the best results in all areas of your life.

If you are not happy with your life, it is up to you to change it.

Chapter 16: The Law of Attraction and Making Choices

As followers of The Law of Attraction, we are taught that action should only be taken after the emotional manifestation has occurred. But what about when a decision must be made before you can be sure of the outcome? Is it possible to make the wrong choice or do the wrong action and mess up your manifestation?

All actions and reactions lead to the same conclusion which is the generation of energy. We manifested into these physical bodies for the purpose of creating life through the generation of this energy. So if the energy we create is relatively negative, it doesn't make a difference in the larger scheme of things. It gives us more things to desire which creates, even more, energy.

The fear of making wrong choices is based on the false notion that we can mess up our manifestation or take it on a grand detour costing us precious time. We also think we only want to experience pleasant circumstances and feel as if we did something wrong if we produce otherwise. So let's clear these misconceptions up.

All choices and actions bring us to a greater understanding of who we are and what we want by not only appreciating what we have but by discovering what we don't want. Do you know anyone who enjoys food poisoning? I don't. When I get to experience it, I want the feeling of relief right away. It generates a lot of energy and can be expressed as making a bad choice. This is where we need to relax our viewpoint a little. I just generated a new and powerful appreciation for feeling healthy. When I return to health, I will feel this new gratitude for a few days. It may even be the launching of a new healthy way of life. It may be just what I needed to refocus on my current fitness goals. Not a bad choice, but a means to an end. Not exactly what we were thinking, but that is the surprise portion that the Universe likes to fill in by itself.

Now for the issue of time. As soon as we are fearful of wasting time, we will produce the events that will help us to waste it. Don't get caught in this trap! Keep the frame of mind, that it comes when it comes and that's perfectly ok. When you relax and allow things to happen in their own sweet time, time will be sweet. Remember what you fight against, what you fear, what you focus on, will always be your dominant vibration and draw to you more of the same.

As for wanting only pleasant experiences, yes, I want that also. I understand and allow everything else because that's all I can do, that's all any of us can do. Energy is just that, energy. Look at it for what it is and it takes the sting out of it. The stronger the energy around an issue the greater the manifestation is going to be. If you can stand back a little and look outside the circumstances to see the larger picture you can catch a glimpse of the power that has just been generated!

Don't hesitate to make choices, or to take action. Speak up, move it and shake it! Generate all the energy you can without fear of errors. Fear is a false notion of you being powerless. You are the power.

Chapter 17: Habits for Happiness

> But what is happiness except the simple harmony between a man and the life he leads?
> ~Albert Camus

It's neither in the things he owns nor in that goal to shed some weight off the scale that can make a man happy. It goes deeper than that. With the complexities that man faces nowadays, it is seldom for one to meet someone who can even give a smile or do something good for a total stranger. Search criminal records and you'd be surprised at seeing that most cases nowadays are due to the pressures of life's problems: from monetary to even their relationships with others. These are people who have grown "depressed" for such low reasons.

Happiness brings that certain glow in a person that can be very influential to many people and not just how he meets with everyday life. It is true that happiness is a choice to make--but it's not by trying to get that object to make us content and all. It's a matter of choice indeed by changing our perspective. Here are tips to liven that mood and can make a person an undeniably "happy person".

1. Show a positive outlook by reaching out and making connections. Friendship even with family members is a good

way of make us happy. It's all about making us feel warm and good inside by making sure that the people we love know how much we care and wish them happy days ahead. Intimate relationships can keep us up and about even at tough times. It's important to keep such connections, one by sending messages, cards or just a simple hug or phone call: "Just saying hi and take care always"...

2. The least we can all do is be thankful. Some people think that they have a lot of misfortunes yet in truth they have more to be thankful for. Either these people end up stressed up that leads them to gain cases in court records or may end up killing themselves (due to hopelessness in life). Make it a habit to start thy blessings; start by appreciating family, next is health, and the rest to even the simplest of thing such as a smile given by someone whom you just passed by. As they say, count thy blessings, not thy misfortunes.

3. Make way to do what you love most. We all have that passion or that thing we love to do most. It may be a hobby like crocheting or photography yet no matter how much you work eight hours a day try to squeeze in a few minutes in doing what something you like. It can be that novel you wish to write (or finish) or getting that Twilight saga novel done before the next movie clip gets into the cinema. Find out ways to make your workday into something exciting.

4. Make do with what you have. Instead of splurging for things to boost that happy meter up during downturns, go for your wardrobe instead. There are a few finds you'd discover: one, in particular, are good pieces to get into those which you've only worn only once or twice. No need to be a shopaholic. You might end up having court records due to your itch for new things.

5. Appreciate simplicity. The best things in life are not those that we see as grand but those that come even as the daily smiles we receive from strangers. It can be the sunlight that touches your skin or that rain that caught you wet on your way home. These are blessings and breather and lessons which say that rain doesn't bring out sorrow, it washes tears away. And even as we search criminal records there are even stories from those involved that end up in a happy ending, even in friendship.

Chapter 18: 5 Ways to Avoid Distractions

Do you find that you start your day refreshed, motivated and raring to go? You take a seat on your computer and somehow the time seems just to slipway?

The day-to-day distractions of life can be very detrimental to your business. If you find that you are disappointed with your productivity at the end of the day, week, the month it can have a massive effect on your future motivation, self-esteem, and productivity.

Here are 5 of the major distractions that life throws at us and how to manage them so that you have a more fulfilling days' work.

1. People - Friends, family, co-workers. All of these people can easily distract you from your daily tasks. With adults and older children, ask them for an uninterrupted block of time. With younger children try to plan your days so that you can work around their daily naps, before they get up or once they have gone to bed.

2. Phone calls and mobile devices - We all know what a distraction these can be. If you need to be a productive turn off all phones. This means no calling no texting no social network

surfing, NOTHING. You will be amazed how much more you achieve in your "mobile free" time.

3. Computer distractions - The urge to just check your social media or have a look at your emails can be strong, but it eats into your day and before you know it your entire morning has gone. If you are working on your computer, disconnect from the internet when you don't need it. Designate specific times to check your emails and close any unneeded browser windows.

4. Environmental Distractions - Ensure that your work environment is free of major distractions. Is it too hot, too cold? Is the television/radio on? Are there other distracting sounds? Is the lighting too bright or too dim? Take actions to overcome any of these distractions before you commence your work.

5. Personal Distractions - Do you need to; walk the dog, make some food, make a drink, pick the kids up? Plan your time accordingly. Make sure that you take care of your personal needs before starting work. Have something to eat but not too much. Eating too much can leave you lethargic and effect your ability to concentrate. Have a drink but don't drink too much, or you will need frequent restroom breaks.

Planning is vital when it comes to avoiding distractions and therefore increasing your productivity. If you keep the above 5 points in mind and plan, accordingly you will see a big improvement in your levels of productivity.

Chapter 19:
Secrets to Get More Done In A Day

Each day as you wake up, a plan is usually laid out on what to achieve on that day. However, many obstacles may hinder one in achieving even a quarter of the laid out plans forcing them to be carried forward. Still, other people plan and finish what is on the list and then get more done even when it was not planned.

Several ways and secrets can be employed to get things done in addition to the ordinary planned. The following can be applied to various things be it in business and day to day running.

First, it is ideal not to start the day by visiting the emails, Facebook or Twitter account. Believe it or not, you might find something which was not planned for and will force you to do unplanned things. This will only generate a bad day by leading one to do things that had not been planned.

When in your workstations, avoid all the unnecessary communications that will distract you like the chatting applications. Your phone should be in a silent mode to avoid obstructions unless you are expecting a very important call. Remember by not being interrupted, not only will you finish the job quickly but also you will do it in a perfect manner.

Set each task with a time limit and work to beat off the time. In case you succeed in finishing the job on time, extra minutes which have been saved will be used to start another job and at the end of the day, you will have achieved to get more done other than the usually listed projects to be completed.

Avoid multitasking. Now many people think multitasking is good. Yes, it is good, and there is the probability of finishing the set goals. However, multitasking is not good when you want to get more done in one day. First, there will be time wastage moving from one item to the next. Secondly one will be too tired and after finishing, there will be no energy to include another job on the day's list.

Delegating some duties to trusted people and workers will get more done. For example, it is possible to hire a qualified person who will finish the jobs on your behalf by paying and supervising them. As you delegate the duties, there will be a big gap at the end allowing one to add an extra duty.

When fulfilling to do list for the day, it is important for a person to start the most important things in the list which cannot be carried forward. Starting off with the hardest task might sound unpleasant, but they are ideal. Ensure that by picking on these tasks; they are bringing the most significant benefits to you.

Make decisions even when they are toughest. Procrastination will and has never paid off and making the toughest decisions will allow one to get more done for the day. When these decisions have been made, then it is time to act on them. The earlier you take the decision, the better it will be for you.

Different jobs and plans need different tactics to finish and get more done. The secret to accomplish more is careful and time management. With this in mind more will be achieved.

Chapter 20: Get More Done in Less Time By Batching Your Tasks

All right already, I admit it! This concept is not new. Nor is it one of my creations. But I have a question for you: are you doing it? Are you leveraging your time by batching your tasks?

Let's break it down.

In a former life...

I'm a former programmer, coder, propeller-head - call me what you will - I use to cut code for money. As a programmer, I was well versed in the idea of batching. We used to queue up our test cases and run them when everyone was asleep. We'd take a truckload of cases and throw them at the system when no one was using it. Then we'd get back the next day and review the results.

Am I losing you?

My point is, we piled it all together and did it in one go. This meant that we didn't have to wait for windows of opportunity. We didn't drag things out. We got a lot done in a small time.

If you're not following, it's probably my fault. Let me explain batching properly: batching is the practice of collecting like tasks together and executing them at the same time. This way you get all of the like tasks completed in one go rather than over an extended period.

Why batching works

The reason batching works is that you are doing the same types of tasks at the same time. There's no back and forth; there're no changing gears. It's all go, go, go. And when you're just going you can get a lot done.

Some obvious examples

Let's look at some rather mundane examples. What about laundry? It would be crazy to wash individual items as they got dirty. So, you wait until there're a full washing basket and them you wash a whole load. What about shopping? You don't get in the car and head to the market every time you need a single item. You wait until your need a bunch of stuff; then you head out. See you're batching already.

Start batching your tasks

So, how else could you batch? Let's think outside the square. Here are some ideas:

Make all of your week's meals in one day. Set aside a few hours every Sunday to make meals that you can refrigerate or freeze.

Pay all of your bills at once. This might take some arranging because you don't want to risk late fees.

Write all of your greetings cards at once. Yes, this sounds crazy, but you're going to forget later. So write all of your birthday, anniversary and Christmas cards at once and then set reminders to mail them.

Batch similar tasks at work. Have to make a lot of calls? Schedule a time and do them all together. Got to write a bunch of articles? Do it at the same time.

Honestly, you can batch just about any groups of tasks that you can think of.

Think outside the square and work out how you can batch your tasks and get more done in less time.

Chapter 21:
Outsourcing -the Right Way to do it

Growing your online business and taking it to the next level requires work. The work you put in doesn't necessarily have to be your own -not when you know how to get others to do it for you. In fact, finding qualified people to do carry out many of your daily tasks is one of the secrets of building your business faster. Hiring more people to work for your business is one way to go about this, but another, more effective option is outsourcing. What's so appealing about outsourcing it which allows you to save both time and money as you delegate many tasks to others. The purpose of this chapter is to give you some insights into effective outsourcing.

If you want to succeed with outsourcing, be sure to make it clear to anyone you interview, that when you set a deadline, you mean it. It's a good idea to stress that you expect your deadline to be met and that the person shouldn't take the job if he or she can't do this. Another issue that's critical is that the freelancer understands exactly what is expected of him/her regarding the job. If you and the freelancer aren't on the same page regarding the job, it will be hard for it to be done by your wishes. Don't take these two factors lightly as they would play a major role in shaping your project. If you feel your candidate doesn't understand them, then simply move on.

One blunder that a lot of online marketers happen to make is that they pick out a vendor, based entirely on their price. While there are no wrongdoings when it comes to staying on top of your investments and cutting costs, you should not snub the other things. If you find a vendor with a good track record, then go for him even if the price is a bit more. If you decide you are going to make an investment, then make it in the correction location. It is easy to fall for vendors that come with a cheap price tag. But your eyes should always be on every single factor including the price.

Many people are perplexed about the differences between hiring someone for a full-time job, which is opposed to outsourcing the work. The truth of the matter is that you should hire anyone this way, whether it is a job or an outsourced project. Checking out a service provider should be done the same way that a job candidate is checked out. This is the greatest way to feel the person. This will provide you with an opportunity to go farther than the standard hiring process for outsourcing. You will not have as many bloopers with outsourcing when you are certain you have had enough time for the hiring process.

When you outsource the task to the right person, you'll feel a lot more relaxed. You can focus better on your strategy and help your business grow. If you get it wrong and hire the wrong person, though, your problems will get immediately bigger. Doing your homework and developing a deep understanding of how outsourcing works will help you out in important ways. It might take you a while to go through all the preparation, but even it'll be worth it. Finding a professional who is willing to take on long-term work and who offers you high quality and timely results are incredibly valuable.

Take Breaks

It's important when striving and going after something to also give ourselves a chance to take breaks. There are different amounts of drive and determination in each of us, but it is crucial that we also keep a healthy balance in our lives. You should spread out responsibilities and time spent with loved ones. Be reasonable about your business, personal, and financial goals. Don't be fantasizing about living in your dream. Live in it. Don't exhaust yourself with your work or mission. Schedule your time and stick to it. Playing with your kids or paying undivided attention to your significant other can be far more beneficial than staring at a computer screen.

We all face writer's block in one way or another. Sometimes our brain just doesn't want to work or focus. It comes down to training ourselves by our schedule. If you work and have a set schedule, tell yourself that those hours you spend at the job are for the job and to focus, pay attention, and devote all your energy to work within those hours. If you don't like your job, schedule an hour after work each day looking for a new one. Some people stress when keeping schedules and making timelines. If that's you then don't schedule, just do something in every area every day.

Do something at work, play with your kids, walk the dog and workout. In every area, strive to accomplish one task and go easy on yourself and be reasonable. Some days you will be tired and some you will just be plain lazy. The important thing is to eliminate stress and balance out your life. We put some crazy deadlines on ourselves sometimes and need to keep things in perspective. We already have enough external pressures. We don't need to become another one to ourselves.

There are times when we need our creativity to work and if it isn't working, go for a quick jog. If something isn't happening for you, do another task not related until something starts to click again. It's like the law of attraction; you look for it, and it doesn't show; you don't look for it and its right there. Stop trying so hard and it will come to you. Tell yourself what you need to do with conviction, believe it, and then give it time to take seed and produce that result you want.

If it comes down to scheduling breaks for you, then so be it. If schedules aren't your thing, go with how you feel. If you feel more productive at a certain hour, but your work schedule isn't on that same schedule, then utilize your creativity to deal with your particular situation. We all need breaks. Sometimes that writer's block is one way to your brain telling you to go for a run.

Conclusion

Thank you again for downloading this book!

I hope this book was able to help you to realize the ways to increase your productivity as well as setting your goals right.

The next step is to put into practice.

Thank you and good luck!

www.ingramcontent.com/pod-product-compliance
Lightning Source LLC
Chambersburg PA
CBHW070330190526
45169CB00005B/1833